AF416085

QUEER BEATS
STORIES FROM LGBTQ+ ARTISTS
IN THE MUSIC INDUSTRY
YOUNG PENNY
True Soundz Entertainment

Queer Beats: Stories from LGBTQ+ Artists in the Music Industry

Young Penny

Published by Top G Records, 2023.

QUEER BEATS: STORIES FROM LGBTQ+ ARTISTS IN THE MUSIC INDUSTRY

First edition. August 15, 2023.

Copyright © 2023 Young Penny.

ISBN: 979-8223725121

Written by Young Penny.

"To Big Freedia, my beloved twerking queen, for inspiring me to tell my truth."

Queer Beats: Stories from LGBTQ+ Artists in the Music Industry

By
Young Penny

Description

From the trailblazing mind of Young Penny, the sensational hip-hop artist who defied norms with hits like 'White Boy Money', 'Fair Casket', and 'Love International', comes a sonic tapestry unlike any other. "Queer Beats: Stories from LGBTQ+ Artists in the Music Industry" is a riveting, no-holds-barred exploration, and a "melodiously penned odyssey through the rhythms of queer representation in the world of music" (East Bay Express).

Young Penny, who shattered ceilings by claiming the title of NYC's first openly gay gangsta rapper, orchestrates an intimate concert of voices, giving readers front-row seats to the symphony of struggles, triumphs, beats, and ballads of the LGBTQ+ community in the music scene. As the maestro of this tale, Penny draws from his own journey, juxtaposing it against the broader crescendo of the queer music movement—each note resonating with tales of love, resilience, activism, and liberation.

Punctuated with vibrant anecdotes and deep reflections, this tome unveils the untold narratives of artists who've danced on the fringes, serenaded from the shadows, and are now stepping into the limelight. It's not just a chronicle of queer music, but a manifesto of self-expression, challenging every reader to find their own rhythm in the cacophony of life.

For fans of Young Penny, music aficionados, and anyone curious about the harmonies of the heart, this book is a ticket to the most evocative concert you'll ever attend. So, turn the pages, feel the pulse, and let the music of 'Queer Beats' transport you.

Foreword

Music - it's the universal language that bridges cultures, eras, and souls. It's also a mirror, reflecting society's evolving norms and values. For many of us who found ourselves in the vibrant yet tumultuous world of the music industry, it's been more than just beats and lyrics. It has been a sanctuary, a platform, and most of all, a voice.

I remember growing up in the pulsating heart of New Orleans, where every street echoed with the brassy notes of jazz and the electric rhythm of Bounce. The city's heartbeat was my lullaby, its streets my playground. But as I navigated the wards of New Orleans, I quickly realized that not all beats were created equal. Some were silenced, some subdued, and some awaiting their moment to explode.

From my earliest days, I was acutely aware of the deep dichotomy that existed. Here I was, a self-proclaimed mama's boy, in a world that often seemed polarized. Amid the underground Bounce scene, the vibrant parades, and the hauntingly beautiful bayous, there was a silent undertone, a hushed narrative waiting to burst forth. The tale of queer artists who were making music not just as a form of self-expression but as an act of defiance and affirmation.

Music became a lifeline for many of us. A space where our identities could unfurl unapologetically. It wasn't just about twerking, wiggling, or shaking to the beats, but about embodying a truth, a reality that mainstream society often shied away from. The underground scenes, the dimly lit clubs, the impromptu street performances - they all became havens for us to be seen, to be heard, and most importantly, to be validated.

Yet, as years turned into decades, a transformation began. The notes that were once hushed began to crescendo. The melodies that were once subdued began to dominate. Artists from all walks of life, from every corner of the world, began to embrace their authentic selves, pushing boundaries and challenging conventions. As they did, the world began to listen, to dance, to celebrate.

This book is a testament to that journey, to that evolution. It encapsulates the passion, the struggles, the triumphs, and the sheer resilience of queer artists in the music industry. As I turned its pages, I saw glimpses of my own journey, of late-night recording sessions, of battling stereotypes, of finding solace in the beats, and of creating a legacy that would resonate with generations to come.

Each chapter is a verse, each artist a note, together composing a symphony that celebrates diversity, love, and authenticity. As a part of this vast tapestry, I've witnessed the highs and lows, the peaks and troughs. From the days when queer music was whispered in the shadows, to today, when it reverberates in arenas, this book encapsulates it all.

To every reader, whether you're an ardent music aficionado, a budding artist, or simply someone seeking to understand the profound depth of the queer narrative in music, this tome is your backstage pass. It invites you to dive deep, to immerse yourself in stories that are not just about music, but about life itself.

As you embark on this journey, remember that each beat, each lyric, each chord is a piece of someone's soul, an echo of their journey. Embrace it, resonate with it, and let the symphony of queer beats become a part of your own life's soundtrack.

And always, always remember: Music knows no boundaries. It only knows love. Let's celebrate that love, one note at a time.

Preface

From the strobe-lit stages of Los Angeles to the pulsating underground clubs of Berlin, my journey in the music world has been nothing short of a rollercoaster. As the proud voice behind hits like 'White Boy Money', 'Fair Casket', and 'Love International', I've had the privilege of watching crowds of all backgrounds vibe to my truths. My name is Young Penny, and my story is as much about beats and rhymes as it is about identity, defiance, and love.

Hip hop has always been a vessel for storytelling, for voicing the unspoken, and for challenging the status quo. When I first dipped my toes into this industry, I was well-aware of the challenges that lay ahead. Being an LGBTQ artist in a genre historically dominated by straight, masculine narratives wasn't just about breaking into the scene—it was about redefining it.

"Queer Beats: Stories from LGBTQ+ Artists in the Music Industry" is more than just an exploration of queer voices in hip hop; it's a testament to resilience, creativity, and the power of authenticity. Inside these pages, you'll find stories that resonate, that inspire, and that challenge preconceived notions of what it means to be queer in the world of beats and bars.

Throughout my career, my identity has both opened doors and erected walls. But every time my song played on the radio or blared from a car passing by, it felt like a revolution—one where love and identity danced hand in hand, unapologetically. It's my hope that by sharing these stories, by shedding light on the experiences of LGBTQ+ artists from different walks of life, we can together amplify the chorus of voices that, for too long, have been relegated to the fringes.

So, whether you're a fellow artist looking for camaraderie, a fan eager to dive deeper into the intricacies of the music you love, or simply someone curious about the interplay of identity and artistry, this book is for you. Welcome to our symphony of queer beats, where every note holds a story, and every story is a call for acceptance and change.

Stay true,
Young Penny.

Introduction

The Queer Soundtrack of a Generation

In the rich tapestry of musical history, each generation seeks its soundtrack, a harmonious blend of melodies and lyrics that encapsulate its spirit, challenges, and victories. However, there exists within this broad soundscape a more specific and deeply resonant beat—a beat that has long hummed in the shadows, sometimes whispered, sometimes shouted, but always persistently pulsing. This is the queer soundtrack of our generation—a collection of rhythms and rhymes that tell tales of love, defiance, identity, and a relentless quest for acceptance.

It's a universal truth that music holds power—a power that transcends language, borders, and, indeed, identities. Within the echoing chambers of this auditory realm, the LGBTQ+ community has found not just solace, but also a medium to voice their unique experiences, dreams, and struggles. To understand the significance of this queer soundtrack, one must first journey back to the days when such voices were suppressed, their melodies stifled, and their stories untold. As the eras shifted, as society's grasp evolved, these voices began to emerge, timidly at first, but with an increasing assertiveness that demanded acknowledgment.

The musical world, as vast and varied as it is, hasn't always been welcoming to those who dared to defy the conventional norms of gender and sexuality. Mainstream genres often confined themselves to tales of heterosexual love, leaving queer narratives to the fringes. However, like water carving its path through rock, these narratives persisted, flowing through underground channels, gathering strength, until they burst forth in a cascade of vibrant soundscapes that the world could no longer ignore.

When one immerses oneself in the queer anthems from the past decades, it becomes evident that these aren't just songs—they're chronicles. Chronicles of clandestine love in times when such affections were a perilous secret, of the spirited rebellion during the AIDS crisis, of the joyful pride in parades where rainbow flags flapped freely in the wind, and of the heart-wrenching pleas for acceptance in a world that often looked askance. In every strum, beat, and lyric, there lies an encapsulated emotion, a fragment of history, a piece of a soul laid bare.

The metamorphosis of the queer soundtrack mirrors the broader evolution of the LGBTQ+ movement. It's no coincidence that as the community garnered more rights, recognition, and representation, their music grew louder, prouder, and more diverse. Today, the industry boasts a plethora of queer artists across genres, each adding their notes to this ever-evolving symphony. From pop to punk, from ballads to beats, the breadth and depth of the queer soundtrack is a testament to the community's multifaceted experiences.

Art, in its myriad forms, often reflects the zeitgeist of its era. And in this current age, where identities are being explored, understood, and celebrated like never before, the queer soundtrack is more than just a reflection—it's a beacon. It beckons listeners to understand, to empathize, and to dance along to the rhythms of lives that might be different, but are as rich, complex, and beautiful as any other.

As we embark on this exploration of the 'Queer Beats', it is essential to approach it not just as a study of music but as a deep dive into the heartbeats of countless individuals who, through their art, have shared their essence with the world. The stories contained within the subsequent pages are not mere biographies or analyses; they're intimate conversations, resonant echoes of the past, and hopeful harmonies of the future.

To truly appreciate the queer soundtrack of our generation, one must listen with more than just the ears. One must listen with the heart, the mind, and the soul. For in doing so, one doesn't just hear music—one experiences a movement, a revolution, a celebration of love in all its splendid forms. As the pages unfold, may you find yourself immersed in this melodic journey, discovering not just the notes, but the stories and spirits behind them.

It's often remarked that the true essence of music, its purest form, resides not just in its harmonies and rhythms but in its stories. The queer community, with its tapestry of experiences, tales of resilience, love, and battles fought, has contributed immeasurably to the pantheon of music. Every chord strummed, every lyric penned down, serves as a chronicle of lives lived on the peripheries, of voices that once whispered in hushed tones but now sing with full-throated abandon.

If one were to take a magnifying glass to the global music scene, one would notice the vibrant splashes of color the queer community has painted on this vast canvas. From underground bars in New York in the turbulent 1960s, where drag queens and queer artists crooned tales of forbidden love, to the glittering stages of global music festivals in the 21st century, where artists proudly proclaim their identities to the accompaniment of roaring applause, the journey has been both tumultuous and triumphant.

While the past held its shadows, where being openly queer could spell the end of a budding musical career, the present tells a more hopeful story. Yet, it would be an oversimplification to state that the music industry is wholly accepting now. There still exist barriers, stereotypes to shatter, and glass ceilings to break. But with every beat that reverberates with pride and every chorus that celebrates diversity, we inch closer to a world where music truly is a universal language, unfettered by biases and prejudices.

To those unfamiliar with the depth and breadth of the queer soundtrack, it might seem like a recent phenomenon, a product of modern liberal thought. In truth, the undercurrents of this movement have been flowing for decades, sometimes subtly and at other times more overtly. The torchbearers of queer music from yesteryears, many of whom faced unimaginable adversities, laid the groundwork for today's artists. They sang not for fame or fortune but for the simple joy of authentic expression, for the solace found in shared experiences, and for the hope that their melodies might someday herald a change.

The modern queer artist stands on the shoulders of these giants. Equipped with a history rich with both pain and pride, they weave narratives that are as much about looking back in gratitude as they are about looking forward with hope. Their music speaks of love in its many shades, of battles both personal and societal, and of the dream of a world where the lines of gender and sexuality blur into irrelevance, leaving behind only the pure, unadulterated joy of existence.

As we delve deeper into the chapters ahead, we shall encounter stories of artists who have not just shaped the queer soundtrack but have also molded the very fabric of the music industry. Their tales are as varied as the genres they represent, but a common thread binds them all – the relentless pursuit of self-expression in a world that often demands conformity. Through their journeys, we will traverse the winding roads of history, art, culture, and identity.

In immersing oneself in these narratives, one finds that the queer soundtrack of our generation is not just for the LGBTQ+ community; it's a clarion call to every individual who has ever felt different, ever felt the need to hide their true self, ever yearned for acceptance. It's a celebration of the human spirit in all its myriad forms and a testament to the power of music to heal, unite, and inspire. So, as we continue our exploration, let's not just listen; let's resonate with the symphony of stories, for in them we might find echoes of our own.

Chapter 1: Setting the Stage

A Brief History of LGBTQ+ Representation in Music

In the grand auditorium of musical history, where each note represents a moment and each song a movement, there lies a section that, for the longest time, played softly, almost imperceptibly. It's the sound of the LGBTQ+ community, whose representation in the music world has been a complex tapestry of subtext, overt declarations, struggles, and triumphs. To truly grasp the nuances of the queer soundtrack of our generation, it's imperative to rewind the tape and set the stage, tracing back the origins of LGBTQ+ representation in music.

As one meanders through the annals of history, the earlier years present a landscape where LGBTQ+ themes and identities in music were cloaked in layers of innuendo and metaphor. The societal milieu of bygone eras, with their rigid norms and stringent codes, meant that artists often had to resort to veiled references, embedding their truths in lyrical ambiguities. Still, even through the haze of these coded messages, the resilience and spirit of the community shone, whispering their tales to those willing to truly listen.

One of the earliest and most notable figures who subtly challenged the status quo was blues singer Ma Rainey, often dubbed the "Mother of the Blues." While her lyrics might have hinted at queer relationships, it was the undertones, the pauses, and the hidden winks that conveyed more than words ever could. Her contemporaries, like Bessie Smith, tread similar paths, with songs that danced on the peripheries of overt queer representation. These pioneers, with their bold performances and suggestive lyrics, laid the foundational bricks for future generations.

As the 20th century progressed, with the world wars casting long shadows and the Jazz Age ushering in winds of change, the music scene began to witness a cautious evolution. The underground LGBTQ+

scene, especially in cosmopolitan hubs, thrived in speakeasies and hidden bars. It was within these safe havens that queer artists and audiences found a space to express and embrace their identities, away from the prying eyes of a judgmental society.

However, the journey wasn't linear. The subsequent decades, with the conservatism of the 1950s and the tumultuous 1960s, presented a dichotomy. On one hand, the broader societal narrative sought to push queer identities back into the closet. On the other, the burgeoning civil rights movements, coupled with the nascent stirrings of LGBTQ+ activism post the Stonewall riots, began to influence the music industry. Icons like Dusty Springfield and later, David Bowie, with their androgynous personas and refusal to adhere to gender binaries, challenged perceptions and redefined norms. Their music, their aesthetics, and their public personas became rallying cries for a generation yearning for change.

The late 20th century marked a significant shift, with the advent of punk rock and its ethos of rebellion against conventional norms. Bands and artists wore their queer identities as badges of honor, making music that was both a reflection of their personal experiences and a broader commentary on society. The Village People, with their flamboyant style, and artists like Freddie Mercury of Queen, with his unparalleled stage presence, brought LGBTQ+ representation to mainstream music. Their songs became anthems, not just for the queer community, but for all who championed the ideals of love, freedom, and self-expression.

Entering the modern era, with the world shrinking into a global village, the rise of pop culture brought with it icons who have been instrumental in propelling LGBTQ+ representation to new heights. Figures like Elton John, George Michael, and more recently, artists like Lady Gaga, Frank Ocean, and Tegan and Sara, have worn their identities with pride, creating music that speaks of love in all its forms. Their impact goes beyond just their songs; their very existence, and the acceptance and adoration they receive, herald a brighter, more inclusive future.

Yet, for all the strides made, the road hasn't been devoid of challenges. Even today, numerous artists across the globe grapple with societal expectations, cultural norms, and industry pressures. Coming out, for many, remains a decision fraught with professional and personal implications. However, the winds of change are undeniable. Streaming platforms, social media, and an increasingly interconnected world have democratized music like never before. Queer artists from diverse backgrounds, genres, and cultures now find platforms to share their stories, reach out to audiences, and more importantly, to resonate with listeners who see reflections of their own journeys in these songs.

The history of LGBTQ+ representation in music is not just a collection of dates, artists, and songs. It's a living, breathing narrative of a community's journey from the shadows to the spotlight. It's a testament to the power of art to challenge, to change, and to champion causes. As we stand on the cusp of a world where boundaries are blurring and old norms are being rewritten, the queer soundtrack of our times serves as a reminder of where we've come from, the battles fought, the victories celebrated, and the harmonious future that awaits.

Chapter 2: Pioneers in Disguise

Early Queer Artists and Their Coded Lyrics

In the vast tapestry of musical history, one might find threads that, at first glance, appear unassuming, but upon closer inspection, reveal intricate patterns and hidden messages. Such is the legacy of the early queer artists, whose very existence in a time of stringent societal norms necessitated the art of subterfuge, of coding their truths in layers of lyricism and artistry. Theirs is a tale of ingenious camouflage, where truths whispered in the dark found their way into the limelight, but always in disguise.

To embark on this journey of musical subtext, we must first transport ourselves to an era where the constraints of society's moral compass were suffocatingly tight. The early 20th century, with its black and white views on gender roles and sexuality, created an environment where queer artists, many of whom were at the pinnacle of their careers, had to tread a delicate balance. Their art, which was a reflection of their soul, couldn't be transparent about their identities or desires without risking backlash, if not outright ostracization.

Take, for instance, the blues movement. Often viewed as the bedrock of modern popular music, the blues, with its raw emotion and soulful melodies, provided the perfect canvas for queer artists to paint their stories. Legends like Ma Rainey and Bessie Smith didn't just croon about the usual tales of lost love and heartbreak. Interspersed within their songs were narratives of queer love and relationships. However, the artistry lay in their delivery. These tales were often hidden in plain sight, layered with double entendres and metaphors that could be deciphered only by those in the know.

Billy Strayhorn, the mastermind behind many of Duke Ellington's hits, is another luminary whose art was intricately tied with his queer identity. While his genius was undeniable, and his contribution to the world of jazz invaluable, Strayhorn's sexuality was a facet of his life he had to shield from the public gaze. The lyrics he penned, however, often contained coded nods to his queer experiences, creating a clandestine bond with those who could read between the lines.

As the decades rolled on, the swing and big band era brought forth new challenges and opportunities. With the world plunged into the chaos of war and the subsequent post-war euphoria, music became both an escape and a commentary. Queer artists of this period, while still navigating the treacherous waters of societal judgment, began to find more spaces where they could be themselves, if only behind closed doors. Their music, too, evolved. The codes became more sophisticated, the metaphors more intricate, and the songs themselves became more than just melodies – they became anthems for the underground.

Consider the enigmatic life of jazz pianist and singer Hazel Scott. Though her marriages to men were well-publicized, whispers about her liaisons with women circulated in close-knit circles. Scott's performances, especially her renditions of popular songs, contained subtle alterations — a shift in tempo here, a lingering note there — which, many speculate, were her way of communicating her layered identity.

The advent of rock 'n' roll and the subsequent birth of pop in the 1960s and 70s brought with it a revolution of sorts. The world was changing, and so was the music. Queer artists of this period had the likes of Bowie and Lou Reed to look up to, pioneers who weren't afraid to challenge gender norms and societal expectations. Yet, even in this period of burgeoning freedom, many artists chose to remain in the closet, fearing the repercussions on their careers. Their songs, however, told a different story. Coded lyrics became the norm rather than the exception, with artists embedding their truths in the fabric of their music.

Reflecting upon this era, it's essential to recognize the immense courage and resilience these artists showcased. In a world that was far from accepting, they chose to share their truths, albeit in veiled forms.

Every song they penned, every performance they gave, was an act of defiance, a subtle middle finger to a society that sought to suppress their identities.

In essence, the early queer artists and their coded lyrics serve as a poignant reminder of the lengths individuals have gone to express themselves authentically. Their legacy, etched in the annals of musical history, is a testament to the indomitable spirit of the LGBTQ+ community. It's a legacy of resistance, of finding light in the darkest of times, and of singing one's truth, even if in disguise. As modern listeners, when we revisit these classics and unearth the hidden stories within, we're not just enjoying music – we're honoring the pioneers who dared to be different and, in doing so, paved the way for future generations.

Navigating through the annals of time, the profound influence of these pioneers becomes even more apparent when we consider the generations that followed. Their ingenuity in crafting lyrics that contained hidden gems of their truth set a precedent, but it also laid the foundation for a more overt form of self-expression that would burgeon in the ensuing decades. The fortitude and resilience displayed by these artists serve as a beacon, guiding those who would later choose to use music as a platform for both personal and societal transformation.

As we transitioned into the 1980s, the world found itself at the precipice of an era characterized by change. Music, always the faithful mirror to society's soul, began to capture the essence of this transformative period. Synth-pop, new wave, and an array of emerging genres became the soundtrack of a generation that was beginning to challenge traditional norms with fervor. While artists like Madonna and George Michael were making waves on the charts, their music also often carried echoes of those that preceded them. Lyrics became bolder, the innuendos less concealed, and the messages more direct. Yet, the influence of the coded lyricism of yesteryears was still palpable.

Amid this backdrop, one can't overlook the profound impact of the AIDS epidemic on the queer community and the music industry at large. With the world grappling with this crisis, music became both a balm for wounded souls and a tool for advocacy. Queer artists who had previously coded their experiences in their lyrics now found a pressing need to be more overt, driven by the urgency of the times. Their songs became rallying cries for compassion, understanding, and change. And while the specter of the disease loomed large, the indomitable spirit of the community, much like the pioneers of the past, shone through.

The 1990s and 2000s saw a further evolution, with the rise of genres like grunge, hip-hop, and indie rock. The musical landscape became a vibrant mosaic, with queer artists making their mark across genres. The legacy of their forebears, those early maestros of coded lyricism, was evident even now. Artists like Ani DiFranco, Melissa Etheridge, and k.d. lang, while more overt in their lyrical content, often employed the subtle artistry of metaphor and allegory, a nod to the pioneers of the past.

In the interconnected world of the 21st century, where barriers were gradually eroding, and the exchange of ideas became instantaneous, the music scene bore witness to a renaissance of sorts. Artists like Janelle Monáe, Frank Ocean, and Tegan and Sara began pushing boundaries, not just musically but also in their lyrical narratives. Their songs, while rooted in their personal experiences, resonated with a global audience, bridging divides and fostering understanding.

Reflecting on the trajectory of queer representation in music, one is struck by the sheer tenacity of the artists who have graced this landscape. From the coded lyricism of the early pioneers to the unapologetic anthems of modern-day icons, the journey has been long and fraught with challenges. Yet, at every juncture, the spirit of resistance, the desire to tell one's story, and the innate human need for authentic self-expression have prevailed.

As we tune into the melodies of today, enriched by the harmonies of the past, it becomes evident that music, in all its forms, has been an unwavering ally of the LGBTQ+ community. The pioneers in disguise, with their lyrical subterfuge, have not only left an indelible mark on the world of music but have also paved the way for generations to sing their truths, loud and clear. Their legacy is one of courage, resilience, and an undying hope for a world where love, in all its myriad forms, reigns supreme.

Chapter 3: Breaking Boundaries

The 80s and 90s: A New Wave of Queer Visibility

The kaleidoscopic decades of the 80s and 90s stand as beacons in the history of music, glinting with the shimmer of innovation and experimentation. More importantly, these years also heralded a new wave of queer visibility in the industry. The constraints of yesteryears, while not obliterated, were being continually challenged, allowing the LGBTQ+ community to carve out spaces of genuine self-expression. Their narrative was no longer confined to whispers; it roared and resounded in anthems and ballads alike.

To understand the profound transformation of these decades, we must recognize the socio-political backdrop against which they unfurled. The 80s were marked by a paradoxical mix of conservative political climates, especially in regions like the U.S., juxtaposed against burgeoning subcultures that challenged the status quo. The advent of MTV and the music video revolutionized how artists expressed themselves, giving them a powerful visual medium to augment their auditory tales.

Amid this explosive milieu, queer artists began to stake their claim, pushing boundaries both musically and visually. Culture Club, with the enigmatic Boy George at the helm, epitomized this transformation. With his androgynous looks and unabashedly queer persona, Boy George became an icon, not just for his musical prowess but for his unflinching challenge to gender norms. Songs like "Karma Chameleon" didn't just top charts; they also subtly tackled themes of identity, love, and acceptance.

Simultaneously, the 80s witnessed the rise of artists like Elton John, George Michael, and Freddie Mercury, who, while not openly out at the start of their careers, played pivotal roles in challenging heteronormative conventions. Their songs, stage performances, and music videos often contained elements that hinted at their true selves. George Michael's "Outside," for instance, was both a brilliant pop song and a defiant response to his arrest for a lewd act, shedding light on his sexuality.

The 80s were also marked by the tragic AIDS epidemic, which disproportionately affected the queer community. As grief and anger welled up, music became a salve, a platform for activism, and a call for compassion. Madonna, while not queer herself, became an ally, using her immense influence to raise awareness and combat the pervasive stigma surrounding the disease.

Transitioning into the 90s, the musical landscape was rife with a plethora of genres, from grunge to Britpop, from R&B to electronic music. As the World Wide Web began to weave its intricate web across the globe, the world became more interconnected, leading to a cross-pollination of musical styles and cultures. The queer community was right at the epicenter of this seismic shift, leveraging these new platforms and channels to amplify their voices.

Artists like k.d. lang, Melissa Etheridge, and the Indigo Girls were open about their sexuality and used their music to address queer themes. lang's "Constant Craving," with its soulful melodies and poignant lyrics, resonated deeply with anyone who'd ever felt the pangs of unrequited love. Concurrently, RuPaul, with his infectious charisma, brought drag culture to the mainstream, challenging and playfully mocking traditional gender roles.

The Riot Grrrl movement of the 90s, with its feminist punk rock ethos, further amplified queer voices. Bands like Bikini Kill and Sleater-Kinney, while primarily known for their feminist messages, also included queer members who infused their music with themes of queer love, identity, and resistance.

Towards the latter part of the 90s, as society edged towards the new millennium, there was a palpable sense of change in the air. With artists like Ani DiFranco and Rufus Wainwright making waves, the boundaries of what was considered 'mainstream' began to blur. The stage was set for an era where artists would no longer be defined solely by their sexuality but by the sheer depth and breadth of their artistry.

The decades of the 80s and 90s were nothing short of revolutionary for queer representation in music. The artists from these eras not only pushed musical and societal boundaries but also laid the foundation for future generations. Their legacies are imprinted in the notes and lyrics of the songs we cherish, in the music videos we replay, and in the cultural shifts they helped orchestrate. The winds of change they set in motion continue to reverberate, reminding us of the power of music to heal, to challenge, and to unite.

Chapter 4: Pop and Pride

The Role of Queer Artists in Mainstream Pop

The effervescent realm of pop music has always been reflective of the zeitgeist, of the prevailing cultural, societal, and political undercurrents. As the years progressed and the world gradually stepped into a milieu more accepting and inclusive, queer artists began to emerge from the shadows, stamping their irrefutable mark on mainstream pop. Their influence wasn't merely confined to chart-topping numbers or sold-out arenas; it permeated deeper, shaping perceptions, challenging norms, and weaving tales of love, loss, and liberation.

Pop music, by its very nature, is inclusive, designed to resonate with the masses. Its infectious beats, memorable melodies, and relatable lyrics have the power to bridge divides, making it an ideal platform for queer artists to share their narratives. As they entered this domain, these artists not only diversified the soundscape but also injected it with tales previously untold in such a vast, mainstream arena.

One cannot embark on a discourse about queer representation in pop without mentioning the inimitable George Michael. While he began his journey with coded lyrics and a carefully crafted image, as the years progressed, he became a symbol of unabashed authenticity. His journey, fraught with challenges, from his days with Wham! to his illustrious solo career, was emblematic of the struggles faced by many queer artists. Yet, songs like "Freedom! '90" resonated universally, encapsulating the human desire for self-expression and liberation.

Following closely on his heels was the meteoric rise of artists like Ricky Martin, whose electrifying performance at the 1999 Grammy Awards propelled him to international fame. When he came out in 2010, he not only affirmed his identity but also underscored the idea that talent knows no bounds of sexuality. His story became a beacon of hope, particularly for queer artists hailing from cultures steeped in traditional norms.

The 2000s saw the ascendancy of queer female artists in mainstream pop. Tegan and Sara, the Canadian twins known for their indie credentials, surged into the pop sphere, bringing with them a unique blend of vulnerability and vivacity. Their songs, while rich in catchy hooks, were also potent tales of queer love, identity, and acceptance.

Yet, it wasn't just individual artists who were making waves. The pop culture phenomenon that was Glee, a television show replete with musical numbers, played a pivotal role in mainstreaming queer narratives. Characters like Kurt Hummel and Santana Lopez, with their struggles and triumphs, were brought to life not just through powerful performances but through songs that echoed their journeys.

As the 2010s unfurled, the pop world was graced by artists like Sam Smith and Troye Sivan, who wore their identities on their sleeves. Their songs were profound narratives of queer experiences, yet they resonated universally. Smith's "Stay With Me" and Sivan's "Youth" became anthems not just for the queer community but for anyone who's ever grappled with the complexities of love and longing.

In the backdrop of these individual success stories was the increasing presence of LGBTQ+ themes in mainstream pop music videos. Taylor Swift's "You Need To Calm Down" stands out as an example, celebrating queer culture and serving as a call against bigotry. Even if not LGBTQ+ themselves, many artists became allies, using their platforms to propagate messages of love, acceptance, and unity.

However, while the progress was undeniable, challenges remained. Many queer artists grappled with the pressure to conform, to fit into marketable molds. Yet, as each artist broke a barrier, they paved the way for the next, ensuring that the path became a tad less arduous for those following in their footsteps.

As we delve deeper into the harmonious fusion of pop and pride, it's imperative to acknowledge the pioneering voices that challenged the industry's conventions. These artists crafted a space for themselves in an ecosystem that often seemed intent on sidelining or silencing them. However, through sheer talent, resilience, and authenticity, they not only carved out niches but also expanded the boundaries of mainstream pop.

Lady Gaga stands tall among these luminaries. Bursting onto the scene in the late 2000s with her avant-garde style and audacious performances, Gaga wasn't just another pop star; she was a movement. Embracing her bisexuality, she became an emblem of hope and pride for countless fans across the globe. Her anthem "Born This Way" was a clarion call for acceptance, reverberating with lines that resonated deeply with the LGBTQ+ community and beyond.

Another influential figure, Hayley Kiyoko, coined as "Lesbian Jesus" by her fans, is emblematic of the newer generation of queer pop artists. Her music videos, rife with queer love stories, were groundbreaking in their candidness and representation. Songs like "Girls Like Girls" and "What I Need" didn't just skim the surface; they delved deep, presenting narratives that were both personal and universal.

Frank Ocean's emergence in the R&B-pop crossover space is another testament to the expanding horizons of queer representation. His letter on Tumblr, where he opened up about his first love being a man, was both a personal revelation and a watershed moment in the world of hip-hop and R&B—a genre space historically not known for its openness to queer themes. Yet, Ocean's songs, laden with emotional depth and musical sophistication, transcended these barriers, earning accolades and love from all quarters.

The growing acceptance of queer artists in mainstream pop was paralleled by increasing representation in events and platforms that celebrated music. The Eurovision Song Contest, a musical extravaganza that garners viewership in the millions, witnessed the crowning of Conchita Wurst, a drag queen with a powerful voice and an even more potent message. Her victory was not just for her musical prowess but was emblematic of the shifting tides in popular culture.

Additionally, the music festivals and tours around the world began to feature a more inclusive lineup of artists. Pride festivals, which celebrated LGBTQ+ culture, were no longer the only venues where queer artists could headline. Major festivals like Coachella, Lollapalooza, and Glastonbury featured queer artists, not as token representations, but as major attractions.

As we stand on the cusp of a new era, with the echoes of the past still reverberating, it's clear that the trajectory of queer artists in mainstream pop is an ascending one. Yet, it's also crucial to remember that this journey wasn't a solitary one. Alongside the artists were fans, producers, and even fellow musicians who became allies, amplifying the message of inclusivity.

The road ahead, while promising, is also laden with responsibility. As more queer artists find their voices, the industry and the listeners must ensure that these voices are heard, celebrated, and cherished. After all, pop music, in its essence, is a reflection of society. As it becomes more inclusive, it not only entertains but also educates, fostering a world where love, in all its myriad forms, is celebrated.

In concluding this exploration, it's evident that the intertwining of pop and pride has been a journey marked by both victories and vicissitudes. Queer artists, with their indomitable spirit, have not only enriched the tapestry of pop music but have also played a pivotal role in shaping societal perceptions. Their stories, encapsulated in three-minute pop songs, serve as reminders of the power of music to reflect, to challenge, and to inspire. As the world hums along to these tunes, it becomes privy to tales of a community that, while diverse in its experiences, shares a universal yearning for love, acceptance, and the freedom to be.

Chapter 5: Rocking the Boat

Queer Representation in Punk, Rock, and Alternative Scenes

In the annals of music history, rock, punk, and alternative genres have always epitomized the spirit of rebellion, a vocal resistance against established norms and conventions. Ironically, while these genres heralded countercultural movements, the representation and acceptance of queer voices within their folds wasn't always a given. However, as history unfolded, the interplay of queerness and these genres resulted in a potent fusion, producing some of the most iconic and transformative musical moments.

The very genesis of rock 'n' roll, a genre that emerged as a harbinger of social change in the mid-20th century, was deeply intertwined with queer culture, even if it wasn't overt. Artists like Little Richard, with his flamboyant style and unabashed performances, hinted at a queerness that might not have been openly acknowledged but was palpable. His song "Tutti Frutti," while seemingly innocuous, was originally penned with risqué lyrics that were subsequently toned down for mainstream audiences. Thus, even in the nascent stages of rock, queer undertones were pulsating, waiting for the right moment to emerge into the limelight.

However, it was the 1970s glam rock movement that truly marked the arrival of queer aesthetics in the rock realm. Artists like David Bowie and Freddie Mercury shattered gender norms with their androgynous looks, fluid personas, and lyrical innuendos. Bowie's Ziggy Stardust persona and his declaration of bisexuality were not just headline-grabbers; they became defining moments in rock history. Mercury, with his unparalleled vocal prowess, led Queen to become one of the most iconic rock bands, all while maintaining an aura of mystery about his sexuality.

Parallel to the glam rock wave was the punk movement, which, in its raw and unapologetic spirit, became a natural ally for queer artists. The punk scene, particularly in cities like New York and London, became havens for LGBTQ+ individuals. Bands like The Buzzcocks and Jayne County & The Electric Chairs explored queer themes in their music. Patti Smith, with her androgynous appeal and profound lyrics, became a seminal figure in the punk rock milieu, hinting at the fluidity of gender and sexuality.

The 1980s saw the alternative rock and indie scenes begin to flourish, carrying forward the legacy of their predecessors. Bands like R.E.M., fronted by the enigmatic Michael Stipe, straddled the worlds of mainstream rock and the alternative scene. Stipe's eventual coming out in the 1990s was less a sensational revelation and more an affirmation of the queerness that had always subtly informed his music.

The riot grrrl movement in the 90s was another turning point. This feminist punk movement, with its roots in the Pacific Northwest, was a clarion call against patriarchy, sexism, and also championed queer rights. Bands like Bikini Kill and Bratmobile, with their fierce lyrics and raucous performances, brought lesbian and queer issues to the forefront of the punk scene.

However, despite these strides, challenges persisted. The world of rock, particularly in its more traditional and heavy sub-genres, was often perceived as a masculine domain, making the acceptance of queer artists an uphill battle. Yet, artists like Rob Halford of Judas Priest, with his powerful vocals and leather-clad persona, proved that sexuality and talent were not mutually exclusive. Halford's coming out in the late 90s was a significant moment, signaling that even in the heavy metal arena, queerness had a place.

As the new millennium dawned, the boundaries between genres became increasingly porous. Queer artists in rock, punk, and alternative scenes no longer felt the need to be pigeonholed. Bands like Tegan and Sara, previously mentioned in the context of pop, showcased their versatility by embracing rock and indie elements. Similarly, artists like Anohni (formerly known as Antony Hegarty) of Antony and the Johnsons, with her ethereal voice, melded alternative rock with themes of gender, identity, and transformation.

In summing up this exploration, it becomes clear that queer representation in rock, punk, and alternative scenes was not a linear journey but a complex interplay of resistance, acceptance, and evolution. The artists who dared to rock the boat were not just musicians; they were trailblazers, carving out spaces in domains where they were often the outliers. Their legacies serve as a testament to the indomitable spirit of music and its ability to transcend labels, offering solace, strength, and inspiration to generations.

Chapter 6: Hip-Hop's Queer Evolution

Navigating and Challenging Norms in Rap and Hip-Hop

Hip-hop, with its origins rooted in the cultural tapestry of New York City's marginalized neighborhoods, has historically been a space where narratives of social resistance, street credibility, and the hardships of urban life interweave. However, when it comes to LGBTQ+ representation within the hip-hop community, the journey has been convoluted, laden with both obstacles and moments of triumphant revelation.

Traditionally, hip-hop and rap carried a perceived masculine bravado, where tales of machismo, toughness, and the trials and tribulations of life in the 'hood' took center stage. This backdrop, while central to the ethos of hip-hop, unwittingly contributed to an atmosphere where expressions of queerness were often relegated to hushed undertones. In such a setting, for an artist to confront or even hint at a queer identity was tantamount to walking a tightrope.

However, as the narrative tapestry of hip-hop began to evolve, with artists using their platforms to address a myriad of issues ranging from political activism to mental health, the dialogues surrounding sexuality and identity began to percolate to the surface. Among the trailblazers who undertook this delicate journey of self-expression, few shone as brightly as Lil Nas X.

Emerging seemingly out of the blue with his crossover hit "Old Town Road," Lil Nas X was initially celebrated for blurring the lines between country and hip-hop. Yet, it was his subsequent revelations about his sexuality, paired with bold musical endeavors such as "Montero (Call Me By Your Name)," that truly solidified his place as a force of change within the hip-hop universe. Using imaginative and often provocative imagery, Lil Nas X unabashedly celebrated his queerness, challenging both fans and critics to expand their perceptions of what hip-hop could encompass.

Tyler, the Creator, another titan of modern hip-hop, approached the theme of sexuality with a nuanced subtlety. Over the course of his storied career, his lyrics often meandered through introspective alleys, leaving breadcrumbs of his personal explorations. By the time Tyler addressed his sexuality more overtly in his album "Igor," he had already laid the groundwork for a multifaceted portrayal of identity. His artistic evolution showcased that queer narratives in hip-hop weren't just about outward declarations but also the intricate inner journey of self-acceptance.

Yet, as we weave through these narratives, it's impossible to overlook the seismic impact of Young Penny, the first openly gay gangsta rapper from NYC. Penny's audacious entry into the hip-hop scene was akin to a storm, challenging conventions at multiple levels. With hits like "White Boy Money" and "Fair Casket," he explored the intersections of street life, gangsta rap, and queerness with an authenticity that was hitherto unseen. Being an openly gay artist in a sub-genre rife with tales of violence, loyalty, and turf wars was in itself revolutionary. But Penny didn't stop at just being a symbol of representation; he brought forth raw narratives that resonated with both the LGBTQ+ community and hardcore hip-hop fans, a testament to his lyrical prowess and genuine storytelling.

In tracks like "Love International," Penny spun tales of love and desire that transcended the gritty streets of New York, hinting at universality in emotions, regardless of sexuality. Such endeavors showcased that, at its core, hip-hop was about storytelling and authentic experiences, and the tales of queer individuals were as integral to this tapestry as any other.

The trajectory of queer evolution within hip-hop, while marked by triumphant moments, wasn't without its challenges. Artists like Lil Nas X, Tyler, the Creator, and Young Penny often faced backlash, not just from conservative sections of society, but occasionally from within the hip-hop community itself. These confrontations, while painful, also led to introspective dialogues about the essence of hip-hop and the space it offered for diverse voices.

Hip-hop's queer evolution is a testament to the genre's intrinsic adaptability and its capacity to mirror societal changes. Artists who dared to challenge and navigate the intricate norms of hip-hop not only expanded its boundaries but also enriched its soul. Through their verses, beats, and lives, they underscored a poignant truth: that hip-hop, in its essence, is a celebration of authentic voices, regardless of where they come from or who they love.

Chapter 7: Harmonizing Identities

Stories of Trans and Non-Binary Artists in the Industry

The musical landscape, as vast and diverse as it might seem, has historically oscillated between waves of acceptance and erasure. While discussions around gay, lesbian, and bisexual representation have gradually gained momentum in recent decades, the narratives of transgender and non-binary artists have been slow to pierce through the mainstream consciousness. This chapter delves deep into the journeys of these artists, exploring their nuanced experiences and the profound impact they've had on the broader musical tapestry.

Transgender and non-binary voices in music are not a new phenomenon. One might be tempted to perceive them as contemporary revelations, but in reality, these artists have been the quiet harmonizers of musical history, often pushed to the margins, yet undeniably present. Their stories are interwoven with resilience, self-discovery, and the unyielding pursuit of artistic authenticity.

One such trailblazing artist who comes to mind is Wendy Carlos, the virtuoso behind the iconic "Switched-On Bach," a groundbreaking album from the late 1960s that brought classical music into the modern era through the Moog synthesizer. Carlos's journey as a transgender woman was as multifaceted as her musical creations. She navigated the complexities of transitioning in a time where understanding and acceptance were sparse. Yet, her indomitable spirit shone through not just in her personal life, but also in her innovative contributions to electronic music.

As the late 20th and early 21st centuries unfurled, a new generation of transgender and non-binary artists began to emerge, each bringing with them unique perspectives and sounds. Anohni, formerly known as Antony Hegarty of the ensemble Antony and the Johnsons, is a radiant example. With a voice that can only be described as ethereal, Anohni's music delves deep into themes of identity, environment, and societal constructs. Songs like "Hopelessness" and "Drone Bomb Me" transcend mere melodic constructs; they are profound reflections on the world's state and the artist's personal journey as a trans woman.

Non-binary artists, too, have carved significant niches in the industry. Artists like Janelle Monáe, with their electrifying presence and genre-defying music, have opened up dialogues on fluidity and the spectrum of gender. Monáe's declaration of being a "free-ass motherfucker" in relation to their sexuality and gender is emblematic of a broader movement within music — one that seeks to decouple the art from rigid labels and classifications.

Tash Sultana, another non-binary powerhouse, brings to the table a mesmerizing blend of reggae, alternative rock, and soul. Their journey, marked by struggles with mental health and drug addiction, also touches upon the intricacies of navigating identity. For Sultana, music became a therapeutic outlet, and their tracks are replete with raw emotion, skill, and an undeniable authenticity.

The challenges faced by transgender and non-binary artists in the music industry cannot be understated. They've grappled with issues ranging from misgendering by the media and peers to lack of representation at major award functions. Yet, the narratives are not all laden with struggle. There are stories of communities coming together, of collaborations that transcend gender, and of fans who find solace in the music and stories of these artists.

Sophie, a transgender electronic music producer and artist, is a testament to this. With tracks that can be described as sonic adventures, she reshaped the contours of pop and electronic music. Tragically, her life was cut short, but her legacy as a trans woman making waves in a competitive industry remains indelible.

The landscape of music, when seen through the lens of transgender and non-binary artists, is a mosaic of stories, sounds, struggles, and successes. These artists, through their very existence and their art, challenge the industry and listeners to expand their horizons, to listen not just with the ears but with the heart. They harmonize identities, weaving together the threads of gender, artistry, and humanity into a rich tapestry that continues to evolve, resonate, and inspire.

While the aforementioned artists have broken significant ground, the industry's expansiveness means that countless others, operating on the fringes of mainstream recognition, offer equally impactful narratives. These stories, woven together, paint a vivid picture of both the challenges and triumphs inherent in navigating the music realm as a trans or non-binary artist.

Mx. Justin Vivian Bond, for instance, is an avant-garde cabaret artist who uses their platform not just for musical expression but also as an active space of advocacy for the trans and non-binary community. Bond's performances often serve as a hybrid between a musical exposition and a political rally, challenging the audience to reassess preconceived notions about gender, identity, and the power structures that underpin them. Their powerful stage presence, paired with an unmistakable vocal prowess, ensures that the message never loses its potency amidst the melodies.

Then there's Shea Diamond, whose sultry tones and poignant lyrics make her a force to be reckoned with in the realm of R&B and soul. As a Black trans woman, Diamond's songs often delve into themes of love, acceptance, and the struggles that accompany being at the intersection of multiple marginalized identities. Her track "I Am Her" is not just a soulful ballad but an affirmation of her existence, resilience, and an ode to countless others like her who strive for visibility and recognition.

Meanwhile, in the world of hip-hop and rap, artists like Quay Dash and Mykki Blanco are pushing the boundaries of what's traditionally been a very heteronormative and cisnormative space. Their lyrics, laden with assertiveness and often a touch of defiance, call out systemic prejudices while also celebrating the sheer joy and liberation of self-expression. Blanco, in particular, with their eclectic mix of punk, rap, and performance art, represents the embodiment of genre and gender fluidity. Their music isn't just auditory but a multisensory experience, pushing listeners to engage with the content on a deeper, more introspective level.

The journey of these artists is more than just about music; it's emblematic of a broader societal movement. Each song, album, or performance is a step towards a world where identity is celebrated in its myriad forms, where artists aren't just boxed into categories but are recognized for the richness and diversity they bring to the table.

Inevitably, these strides forward are met with resistance. The backlash is often severe, stemming from both institutionalized prejudices and individual bigotry. Yet, what stands out isn't the adversity, but the resilience. Time and time again, trans and non-binary artists have showcased an ability to rise above hate, to use music as both a shield and a spear in their battles.

As we move forward, it's crucial to recognize that the stories highlighted in this chapter are but a fraction of the vast universe of trans and non-binary voices in the music industry. From underground indie circuits to global stages, these artists are crafting a new narrative, one that is rich, diverse, and utterly transformative. Their contributions underscore the idea that music, at its core, is a universal language, transcending barriers of gender, race, and identity. And in this symphony of voices, the notes of trans and non-binary artists ring out loud, clear, and unapologetically authentic.

Chapter 8: Global Queer Beats

LGBTQ+ Music Scenes from Around the World

In our exploration of the queer musical landscape, it's essential to acknowledge that the tapestry of LGBTQ+ representation in music isn't merely a Western construct. The melodic echoes of queer identities resonate globally, with each region offering its own unique inflections and stories. From the sultry tango halls of Buenos Aires to the bustling pop stages of Seoul, LGBTQ+ artists have shaped and been shaped by diverse cultural, political, and social landscapes. This chapter is a voyage into the global queer beats, a celebration of diversity and an acknowledgment of the varied struggles and triumphs of LGBTQ+ musicians across continents.

Our journey begins in Latin America, a region often characterized by its fiery passions and intricate dance rhythms. While countries like Brazil and Argentina are celebrated for their carnivals and tangos, they're also home to a burgeoning queer music scene. Take, for instance, Liniker e os Caramelows from Brazil, fronted by the captivating trans woman Liniker Barros. Their songs, a blend of samba, soul, and R&B, touch upon themes of love, identity, and the struggles of being queer in a society often steeped in machismo. In Argentina, the country that birthed the tango – a dance form traditionally entrenched in heteronormative roles – queer artists are redefining the narrative. Artists like Dani Umpi offer a fresh, unapologetically queer perspective to the rich tapestry of Latin music, seamlessly blending electronic, pop, and traditional sounds.

As we move across the Atlantic to Africa, the narrative takes a slightly different tone. The continent, with its vast array of cultures, languages, and traditions, offers a rich musical palette. Yet, in many African countries, LGBTQ+ rights are still heavily contested, making the act of queer artistic expression both an act of bravery and resistance. In South

Africa, Umlilo, a genre-defying queer artist, challenges societal norms with their eclectic mix of traditional African sounds, electronic beats, and poignant lyrics. Meanwhile, in countries where homosexuality is still criminalized, many artists choose anonymity, using music as a subversive tool to challenge oppressive regimes.

The story in Asia is equally multifaceted. In the sprawling metropolises of Tokyo and Seoul, the pulsating beats of pop music dominate the soundscape. Queer representation in these industries, especially K-pop, has been historically subtle, with artists often resorting to coded language and symbolism. However, the winds of change are palpable. Take Holland, for example, the first openly gay K-pop idol who's challenging the status quo with his unabashedly queer music videos and lyrics. In India, where Section 377, which criminalized homosexual acts, was repealed only recently, artists like Pragya Pallavi are on the forefront of the queer music scene, blending traditional Indian sounds with contemporary beats to craft a unique soundscape.

Europe, with its progressive stances on LGBTQ+ rights in many countries, has been a fertile ground for queer musical expression. From the iconic Eurovision Song Contest, which has seen performances from transgender and drag artists like Dana International and Conchita Wurst, to the underground queer punk scenes in cities like Berlin, the continent is a melting pot of sounds, identities, and stories.

The global journey of queer beats underscores a universal truth: music is a powerful tool of expression, resistance, and celebration. The experiences of LGBTQ+ artists from around the world, while diverse, share common threads of resilience, authenticity, and the unyielding pursuit of self-expression. As borders become more porous and cultures continue to intersect, the future promises an even richer, more inclusive global queer soundscape, echoing with the harmonies of diversity and unity.

In Oceania, the indigenous sounds blend with contemporary beats to produce a unique musical landscape. New Zealand and Australia, with their growing acceptance of LGBTQ+ rights, have seen an explosion of queer artists onto their music scenes. Tash Sultana, an Australian singer-songwriter and multi-instrumentalist, identifies as non-binary and has become a global sensation, blending reggae with rock and soul. Their music speaks to the universality of human experience, transcending boundaries and resonating with listeners worldwide. Meanwhile, New Zealand's Jaimie Webster Haines, a celebrated transgender jazz musician, uses her art to shine a light on the intersection of gender identity and indigenous heritage.

Crossing the Pacific, the islands of the Caribbean have their own rich tapestry of sound, influenced by African rhythms, European colonial history, and indigenous traditions. The LGBTQ+ narrative here is complex, with some nations embracing queer rights while others grapple with deeply ingrained prejudices. Yet, even in this challenging environment, queer artists rise. Diana King, the Jamaican singer best known for her 90s hit "Shy Guy," came out as lesbian in 2012, making her one of the first major Jamaican artists to do so. Her courage paved the way for younger Caribbean musicians to express their truths in their artistry.

Back in North America, while the United States and Canada boast vibrant LGBTQ+ music scenes that often dominate global charts, it's crucial to acknowledge the queer voices from the indigenous communities. Artists like Jeremy Dutcher, a Two-Spirit Wolastoqiyik member, not only revive ancient indigenous sounds in their music but also infuse it with themes of identity, gender, and resistance. Their work reminds listeners of the layered histories and identities that exist within the broader queer narrative.

It's crucial to understand that the global queer beats aren't just about chart-topping hits or the most innovative music videos. They are about underground artists performing in secret venues in countries where their very existence is a defiance. It's about coded lyrics and hushed concerts in basements, where the sound of a guitar string or the beat of a drum becomes a symbol of rebellion. It's about queer nightclubs in bustling cities where the DJ's tracks become anthems of liberation.

These beats also echo in the silent pauses between notes, in the whispered stories of love and loss, in the spaces where artists must tread lightly. They resonate in the claps of audiences, both vast and small, in the tears of a fan who sees themselves reflected in a song for the first time, in the collective voices raised in chorus at a concert.

Each region, each country, each city, and each artist adds a note to this global symphony. The variations in melody, rhythm, and harmony reflect the vastness of the LGBTQ+ experience. Yet, the underlying theme remains consistent: a relentless pursuit of self-expression, authenticity, and love.

As listeners, as we journey through these global queer beats, we're reminded of the power of music. It's not just a form of entertainment but a testament to humanity's capacity for empathy, understanding, and unity. In a world that often feels fragmented, the stories and songs of LGBTQ+ artists from around the globe offer a beacon of hope, a promise of a future where love, in all its diverse forms, plays the leading tune.

Chapter 9: Love, Loss, and Liberation

The Emotional Journeys Expressed in Queer Ballads and Anthems

Throughout the annals of musical history, the narrative of love, with its heartbeats and heartbreaks, has played a pivotal role in shaping and echoing humanity's emotional canvas. Love songs have caressed the ears of listeners across generations, giving voice to their most intimate sentiments. The songs of loss have resonated with the deep pangs of grief, providing solace in moments of solitude. Anthems, on the other hand, have galvanized movements, uniting voices in causes larger than the individual. In the queer realm, these musical genres are imbued with an additional layer of profundity, amplifying experiences unique to the LGBTQ+ community while resonating with the universal emotions of love, pain, and empowerment.

The ballad, by its very essence, is a storytelling medium. Its lyrical depth allows it to delve into the intricate tapestry of emotions, exploring everything from the giddy euphoria of new love to the heart-wrenching pain of separation. Queer ballads, in particular, have been instrumental in capturing the nuances of love that lies outside the conventional heteronormative spectrum. Take, for instance, the ethereal tracks of artists like Perfume Genius or the evocative tunes of Tegan and Sara. Their ballads, steeped in raw emotion, traverse the spectrum of queer love, shedding light on relationships that were, for the longest time, relegated to the shadows. Through their verses, they share tales of clandestine romances, of the thrill of self-discovery, and the anguish of unrequited love, all set against a backdrop that often doesn't recognize or legitimize these feelings.

Loss, as a theme, finds its voice in many queer ballads. But the losses sung about are not merely romantic; they encompass broader themes of identity, acceptance, and the ongoing battle for rights. The heartbreaking ballad "Sylvia" by The Antlers narrates the poignant story of a transgender individual grappling with societal rejection. Such tracks don't merely evoke tears; they offer a somber reflection on the trials faced by the LGBTQ+ community, the personal battles fought in the face of societal prejudice, and the deep-set scars that such struggles leave behind.

Yet, from the depths of pain and struggle, arises the indomitable spirit of the anthem. The queer anthems, in particular, have been more than just songs; they've been battle cries, rallying calls, and declarations of unapologetic selfhood. Who can forget the power of Gloria Gaynor's "I Will Survive"? While not explicitly queer, its resilience-laden lyrics resonated deeply within the LGBTQ+ community, becoming an emblematic track for many during the tumultuous years of the AIDS epidemic and the ongoing fight for queer rights. Similarly, Lady Gaga's "Born This Way" emerged as a modern-day queer anthem, celebrating the spectrum of sexualities and identities. The power of the anthem lies in its universality, uniting voices across divides and sending forth a message of hope, strength, and unwavering pride.

The journey from ballad to anthem encapsulates the very essence of the queer experience. From whispered secrets in dimly lit rooms to bold declarations on bustling streets during Pride parades, the trajectory mirrors the evolution of the LGBTQ+ movement. Love, in all its shades, finds expression in these melodies. The pain of loss, both personal and collective, serves as a somber reminder of the trials faced. Yet, it's the anthems, with their rousing beats and empowering lyrics, that encapsulate the spirit of the community—a community that, despite all odds, continues to rise, love, and thrive.

Such is the power of music; it becomes more than just a collection of notes and rhythms. It transforms into a living testament to human emotion, a chronicle of experiences both singular and shared. The queer ballads and anthems, in particular, serve as an aural history of a community's heartbeats, tears, and triumphant roars. As the world continues to evolve, with more spaces becoming inclusive and accepting, these songs will remain immortal, echoing the tales of love, loss, and liberation that defined, and continue to shape, the queer narrative.

In further examining the realm of queer ballads and anthems, it's essential to consider the broader societal context within which they arise. It isn't just the emotion, the melody, or the voice; it's also about the time, the place, and the cultural milieu. Ballads and anthems are, in many ways, reflections of the zeitgeist, capturing the pulse of the era and the collective consciousness of the community.

An indelible part of the queer narrative is the covert expression of love and desire, often necessitated by societal constraints. Many LGBTQ+ individuals found solace in songs that, while not overtly queer, hinted at feelings and experiences outside the mainstream narrative. Tracks like Dusty Springfield's "You Don't Have to Say You Love Me" or the soulful melodies of Little Richard were rife with subtext, often resonating deeply with queer audiences, allowing them to see glimpses of their stories in between the lines.

The latter part of the 20th century saw a significant shift. As the LGBTQ+ rights movement gained momentum, so did the explicitness and clarity of its musical expression. The ballads of this era were imbued with a raw honesty, a candid exploration of queer love, pain, and aspiration. Songs like k.d. lang's "Constant Craving" broke away from coded language, weaving tales of lesbian longing and desire. Such ballads played a crucial role in normalizing LGBTQ+ narratives, rendering them visible and tangible in the public domain.

Yet, even in these expressions of love and yearning, the specter of loss was never far behind. The AIDS epidemic, which cast a long and devastating shadow over the queer community, found poignant reflection in music. Ballads from this era, such as Bronski Beat's "Smalltown Boy," captured the heart-wrenching experiences of alienation, prejudice, and the palpable pain of loss. These songs served as collective laments, encapsulating the grief of an entire community, mourning the premature loss of so many of its members.

However, intertwined with this tapestry of love and loss are the threads of resilience, strength, and defiance, giving rise to some of the most iconic queer anthems. "Freedom! '90" by George Michael was not just a song; it was a clarion call, an unshackling from societal norms, and a bold embrace of one's true self. Similarly, the pulsating beats of Erasure's "A Little Respect" became synonymous with the plea for acceptance, recognition, and, indeed, a bit of respect.

The significance of such anthems goes beyond their catchy hooks and foot-tapping rhythms. They played, and continue to play, a seminal role in shaping the socio-cultural narrative. By forging a sense of collective identity, these anthems galvanized communities, providing the soundtrack for numerous Pride marches, rallies, and protests. They serve as reminders of the community's strength, its ability to overcome adversity, and its unyielding spirit.

The vast expanse of queer ballads and anthems offers listeners a profound journey through the corridors of history, emotion, and collective experience. From the hushed undertones of hidden desires to the loud proclamations of pride and identity, these songs have charted the evolution of the LGBTQ+ community, capturing its trials, tribulations, joys, and jubilations. They stand testament to the community's indomitable spirit and its relentless pursuit of love, acceptance, and liberation. As future generations look back, these ballads and anthems will serve as poignant markers, melodies that not only entertained but also enlightened, empowered, and eternally echoed the heartbeat of a community.

Chapter 10: Sound and Activism

How Queer Artists Use Their Platform for Change

The transformative power of music has long been acknowledged, transcending mere auditory enjoyment to become an influential conduit for societal change. This influence has been particularly prominent within the LGBTQ+ community, where music and activism intertwine, facilitating a platform for queer artists to voice, advocate, and effectuate change. Through melodies, rhythms, and lyrics, these artists have not only expressed their identities but have also channeled their voices towards broader socio-political causes, leveraging their platforms to challenge norms, inspire movements, and champion inclusivity.

The relationship between sound and activism within the queer community is not a recent phenomenon. Historically, music has often served as the backdrop against which numerous social movements have evolved. From clandestine underground clubs where the LGBTQ+ community found solace and acceptance to global stages where artists advocate for equality and rights, music has consistently played a pivotal role in amplifying the narratives of the marginalized and challenging heteronormative paradigms.

Take, for instance, the rise of the disco era in the 1970s. On the surface, disco may appear as an effervescent musical genre characterized by its pulsating beats and glittering ballrooms. However, delve deeper, and one discerns its revolutionary essence. Discotheques and nightclubs became sanctuaries for the LGBTQ+ community, spaces where they could unapologetically express themselves, free from the prying eyes of a predominantly heteronormative society. These spaces not only fostered self-expression but also germinated seeds of activism. The exuberant dance floors became grounds for mobilization, uniting the community and setting the stage for organized resistance against discrimination and prejudice.

As the socio-political climate evolved, so did the activism embedded in the music. The 1980s, marked by the devastating AIDS epidemic, witnessed artists channeling their anguish, despair, and protest through their tracks. From songs like "Streets of Philadelphia" by Bruce Springsteen that captured the poignant realities of AIDS to tracks that called out governmental apathy, music became a potent tool of advocacy. It humanized the epidemic, moving it beyond statistics and bringing to the forefront the personal stories of grief, resilience, and hope.

The subsequent decades saw queer artists utilizing their platforms with increased vigor, challenging not just homophobia but intersecting issues of racism, gender discrimination, and socio-economic disparities. Artists like k.d. lang, Melissa Etheridge, and later figures like Janelle Monáe and Frank Ocean, used their music to address, question, and defy established norms. Their songs were not just melodic experiences; they were potent political statements, testimonies of their lived experiences, and calls to action for greater inclusivity and acceptance.

The 21st century ushered in a new wave of queer activism, characterized by its global scope and digital prowess. Queer artists, empowered by digital platforms and social media, began reaching audiences across continents. Their messages, rooted in activism, found resonance amongst diverse communities. Artists like Tegan and Sara, with their foundation, leveraged their fame to advocate for LGBTQ+ rights and health. Lady Gaga, with her anthem "Born This Way," and her subsequent Born This Way Foundation, exemplified the fusion of music and activism, promoting mental health awareness, and championing the cause of LGBTQ+ youth.

In today's digital age, the amalgamation of sound and activism has expanded beyond traditional mediums. Social media campaigns, online movements, and digital collaborations have given queer artists the tools to amplify their messages exponentially. Platforms like YouTube, Twitter, and TikTok have democratized activism, allowing emerging queer artists to share their stories, mobilize support, and challenge systemic prejudices.

The interplay between sound and activism within the queer realm underscores the transformative potential of music. It's not just an art form; it's a vehicle of change, a medium that carries within its notes and lyrics the aspirations, struggles, and triumphs of a community. As history unfolds and societal dynamics shift, queer artists, armed with their melodies and messages, will undoubtedly continue to be at the forefront of advocacy, harnessing the power of their platforms to effectuate change, inspire generations, and foster a world rooted in equality, respect, and love.

Chapter 11: Behind the Scenes

Queer Producers, Songwriters, and Industry Shapers

While the limelight often illuminates the performers on stage, shaping the very face of the music industry are countless unsung heroes who work tirelessly behind the curtains. Queer producers, songwriters, and other industry shapers have played an instrumental role in sculpting the soundscape of modern music. Their contributions, although less visible than the artists they support, are vital, weaving the intricate tapestry of sounds, narratives, and emotions that listeners around the globe resonate with.

The queer community's relationship with the music industry extends far beyond the realm of performers. Historically marginalized, many queer individuals found solace and expression not just on the stage but in the recording studios, at mixing consoles, and behind writing desks. These spaces provided them with the canvas to articulate their unique perspectives, experiment with avant-garde soundscapes, and challenge the conventional paradigms of music production and songwriting.

Let's first shine a light on the realm of production. In a domain often dominated by heteronormative perspectives, queer producers brought with them a fresh sonic palette. Their experiences, often characterized by duality - both the celebration of identity and the challenges of societal marginalization - translated into innovative production techniques. Their sounds often straddled the boundary between the mainstream and the alternative, introducing audiences to eclectic mixes, groundbreaking beats, and avant-garde arrangements. Producers such as SOPHIE, whose hyperkinetic sounds have been seminal in pushing the boundaries of pop and electronic music, have redefined what it means to be a producer in the modern music era.

Songwriting, another cornerstone of the music-making process, has witnessed significant contributions from queer individuals. From the poignant ballads capturing the heartaches and elations of queer love to anthems rallying for rights and acceptance, the lyrical landscape has been enriched by the diverse experiences of LGBTQ+ songwriters. Their narratives, often deeply personal, have resonated with broad audiences, bridging gaps and fostering understanding. Queer songwriters like Justin Tranter, who has penned hits for artists ranging from Selena Gomez to Imagine Dragons, have subtly interwoven queer narratives into mainstream music, gently nudging societal consciousness towards greater acceptance and inclusivity.

Yet, the influence of queer individuals extends beyond production and songwriting. They've made significant strides in areas like music video direction, choreography, management, and other pivotal roles that shape an artist's career and public image. Their innovative visions and perspectives have often rendered music videos, performances, and promotional strategies more inclusive and groundbreaking. These professionals have been instrumental in ensuring that the representation of queer narratives isn't limited to lyrics or beats but permeates every facet of an artist's public persona.

Moreover, the industry's evolution would be incomplete without acknowledging the LGBTQ+ music executives who've navigated the boardrooms, advocating for more inclusive policies, artist rosters, and marketing strategies. Their efforts have been pivotal in ensuring that the industry, traditionally seen as a bastion of heteronormativity, evolves to reflect the rich tapestry of human experiences and identities.

In retrospection, while the dazzling world of music often focuses on the artists delivering electrifying performances or chart-topping hits, it's crucial to recognize the cogs in the machine, the unsung heroes behind the scenes. The queer producers, songwriters, and industry shapers have not just contributed to the sounds and narratives but have played a quintessential role in the industry's metamorphosis. Their contributions, echoing with the cadences of love, struggle, acceptance, and pride, have indelibly etched themselves into the annals of music history. They serve as a testament to the fact that the soul of music isn't just in the melodies that caress our ears but in the myriad of hands and minds that craft, nurture, and propel it into our hearts.

Chapter 12: The Digital Era

Queer Visibility in Streaming, Social Media, and Beyond

The dawning of the digital age, marked by the proliferation of the internet, smartphones, and an intricate web of interconnected platforms, has redefined the paradigms of visibility, outreach, and representation. For the queer community, this era of digital evolution has heralded unprecedented opportunities and challenges, reshaping the contours of queer visibility in the sprawling realms of streaming, social media, and the vast digital landscape that lies beyond.

At the forefront of this digital revolution lies the dynamic world of streaming platforms. With juggernauts like Spotify, Apple Music, and Tidal commandeering the music industry's digital frontier, artists have been endowed with a platform that transcends geographical, cultural, and societal boundaries. For queer artists, this has meant a gateway to global audiences, unrestrained by the traditional gatekeepers of the music industry. Emerging LGBTQ+ musicians, who might have once grappled with the constraints of mainstream record labels and radio stations, now find themselves empowered, their voices echoing across continents, resonating with listeners who find solace, joy, and reflection in their tracks. Streaming platforms, with their curated playlists like "Pride Anthems" or "Queer Pop," have not only amplified queer voices but have also woven them into the very fabric of mainstream music.

Yet, the digital landscape's expansiveness isn't limited to streaming alone. Social media platforms - Twitter, Instagram, TikTok, to name a few - have metamorphosed into arenas where queer artists and their fandoms interact, mobilize, and coalesce. The immediacy and intimacy afforded by these platforms have engendered a new form of celebrity-fan relationship, characterized by its authenticity, directness, and reciprocity. For queer artists, platforms like Twitter offer not just promotional avenues but spaces for advocacy, activism, and community building. Whether it's leveraging their influence to rally for LGBTQ+ rights, sharing personal narratives that challenge societal norms, or simply fostering a sense of community among queer fans – social media has emerged as a potent tool in the hands of queer artists.

Beyond music and direct interactions, the digital realm has also witnessed the proliferation of podcasts, YouTube channels, and other content formats that delve into queer narratives. Artists and influencers dissect their experiences, delve into the intricacies of queer representation in the music industry, and foster dialogues that were once relegated to the fringes. These platforms, characterized by their informality and authenticity, have facilitated deeper dives into topics that were once considered taboo, from the challenges of navigating the music industry as a trans artist to the intersectionality of being queer and a person of color.

However, while the digital era has undoubtedly amplified queer visibility, it's not devoid of challenges. The vastness of the internet means that queer artists often grapple with heightened scrutiny, cyberbullying, and the pressures of maintaining a curated online persona. Navigating this digital terrain requires resilience, adaptability, and a discerning approach to the opportunities and pitfalls that lie within the binary code of the digital world.

In reflection, the digital era, in its myriad of forms, has revolutionized queer representation in music. It has democratized platforms, allowing artists to bypass traditional gatekeepers, reach global audiences, and authentically articulate their narratives. The symbiosis between the queer community and the digital realm underscores the transformative potential of technology, highlighting how bits and bytes, algorithms, and online platforms can catalyze societal change, fostering a world where every voice, irrespective of its timbre or cadence, finds an echo. It's an era where the queer narrative, in all its hues and tones, gets woven into the global soundtrack, resonating with clicks, streams, likes, and shares, in a world that's constantly evolving, one digital note at a time.

Chapter 13: Backlash and Resilience

Facing and Overcoming Industry Discrimination and Hate

As with any revolution, the rise and mainstream integration of queer voices in the music industry have been met with an intricate tapestry of both applause and disdain. The narrative of queer artists and industry shapers is as much about the radiant beams of acceptance as it is about the shadowy contours of discrimination, hate, and prejudice. This chapter delves deep into the trenches of the industry's backlash against LGBTQ+ representation, but more significantly, it chronicles the indomitable spirit of resilience that has characterized the queer community's journey in the sonic world.

Historically, the music industry, despite its ostensible veneer of inclusivity and progressiveness, has been rife with instances of overt and covert discrimination against queer artists. This has manifested in a myriad of forms, from record labels shying away from signing openly LGBTQ+ artists, fearing market unacceptability, to mainstream radio stations eschewing tracks that explicitly touch upon queer love or experiences. Such insidious forms of discrimination have often been guised under the cloak of market dynamics or audience preferences, but at their core, they epitomize a deep-seated reluctance to disrupt the heteronormative status quo.

Apart from institutionalized discrimination, many queer artists have faced direct and often virulent forms of hate, both from within the industry and from the larger public. Concerts have been picketed, albums boycotted, and artists subjected to vile vitriol on public platforms. The rise of the digital era, while amplifying queer voices, has also paradoxically magnified the channels for hate. Social media, with its propensity for virality, has often been weaponized to target queer artists, subjecting them to an incessant barrage of hate comments, threats, and discrimination.

However, while the backlash has been formidable, the narrative of queer resilience has been nothing short of awe-inspiring. Artists and their legions of supporters have repeatedly rallied against discrimination, using both art and activism as tools of resistance. The response to hate has often been met with music that is louder, prouder, and unapologetically queer. Tracks that embrace LGBTQ+ identity and love, far from being suppressed, have climbed charts, reverberating across stadiums and earphones alike, a testament to the adage that art, in its purest form, always finds its audience.

Queer artists, rather than being deterred by industry discrimination, have frequently used it as a catalyst for innovation. Independent music labels, queer-centric music festivals, and LGBTQ+ artist collectives have sprouted across the industry landscape. These spaces, founded on principles of inclusivity, acceptance, and representation, have not only provided queer artists with platforms to express themselves but have also profoundly challenged and expanded the industry's horizons.

The resilience narrative also extends to fans and allies of the queer community. Crowdfunded projects, fan-driven campaigns, and grassroots movements have mushroomed in support of LGBTQ+ artists facing discrimination. This groundswell of support, often mobilized digitally, has been instrumental in countering hate, showcasing the power of collective resistance.

In retrospection, the journey of queer representation in the music industry is emblematic of the larger LGBTQ+ movement - marked by peaks and valleys, applause and antagonism, acceptance and aversion. However, the underlying current of this journey has been the unwavering spirit of resilience. It's a narrative of artists who, when told to lower their volume, chose instead to amplify their voices; of fans who, when confronted with hate, chose love and solidarity; of an industry that, when faced with the choice between regression and revolution, saw segments choosing the latter. It's a testament to the enduring power of music, the universal language of love, acceptance, and resistance, echoing through time, breaking barriers, and healing souls.

Chapter 14: Collaborative Queerness

Iconic Collaborations and Queer Anthems of Unity

In the vast and variegated tapestry of music history, there emerges a strand of songs and collaborations that stand out not merely for their melodic beauty or lyrical genius but for their symbolic power. They are the anthems of unity, the collaborative efforts that bind different voices, experiences, and identities into a cohesive, resonant whole. Within the queer musical movement, these collaborations assume an even more profound significance, reflecting a diverse community's yearning for representation, acceptance, and above all, unity. This chapter seeks to immerse itself into the rich waters of these iconic collaborations and anthems, charting their evolution, impact, and the undying spirit of collaborative queerness they encapsulate.

When pondering the realms of queer collaborations, one is instantly drawn to the collaborative efforts that brought together queer and ally artists. These efforts often transcended mere musical partnership, emerging as powerful statements against discrimination and for inclusivity. Think of the anthems that filled pride parades, clubs, and quiet rooms alike, reverberating with messages of love, defiance, and hope. Such collaborations became not just chart-toppers but the soundtracks to countless queer lives and their allies.

The emergence of these collaborations often arose from a mutual respect between artists, recognizing the power of combined voices. When queer artists, often emerging from the shadows of marginalization, joined forces with established mainstream artists, the resulting symphonies were not just musically rich but socially transformative. They served as implicit endorsements, affirmations of the queer community's validity, and challenges to the traditionally heteronormative musical landscape.

To delve into specifics, consider the collaborations that have marked the past few decades. Artists from various genres, backgrounds, and orientations came together, producing tracks that are now emblematic of the queer movement's ethos. These weren't just fleeting partnerships but sustained endeavors, often blossoming into album-length projects or recurrent collaborative ventures. The magic of these collaborations lay not just in their sonic quality but in the narratives they wove, stories of love that defied norms, of identities that refused to be boxed, and of a community's undying spirit.

However, as much as these collaborations celebrated unity, they were also reflective of the queer community's internal diversity. Collaborations weren't just about LGBTQ+ artists and their allies; they were also about queer artists from different orientations, backgrounds, and experiences coming together. When a trans artist collaborated with a gay rapper, or when a bisexual singer-songwriter joined forces with a lesbian rockstar, the resulting music was a celebration of the community's multifacetedness. It was a powerful testament to the fact that while the LGBTQ+ community may be bound by shared struggles and aspirations, it is also characterized by a rich internal diversity.

And then, of course, there are the anthems – songs that might not necessarily be the product of collaborations but became emblematic of the community's ethos. These anthems, often played at pride parades, LGBTQ+ events, or even quiet gatherings, became the rallying cries for a community in its perennial quest for love, acceptance, and rights. They were the songs that queer individuals and their allies sang in unison, finding in their lyrics and melodies, solace, strength, and solidarity.

The story of collaborative queerness is not just about musical partnerships; it's about an ethos, a spirit that recognizes the power of collective voices. It's about understanding that while individual experiences and struggles might vary, there is an underlying thread of shared humanity, aspiration, and love. Through collaborations and anthems, the queer musical movement has showcased the beauty of unity in diversity, crafting symphonies that will echo through time, reminding future generations of the power of love, unity, and collaborative queerness.

Conclusion

The Future Sound of Queer Music

As the final notes of our exploration into the rich and diverse world of queer music fade, we are left with a symphony that is both a reflection of the past and an anticipation of the future. The tapestry of LGBTQ+ sounds, voices, and narratives we've journeyed through is not merely a testament to the community's resilience and vibrancy but is also a harbinger of the melodies yet to come. As we stand on this precipice, gazing into the future sound of queer music, there are both assurances and aspirations, certainties and curiosities.

The first and foremost assurance is continuity. The LGBTQ+ community, having carved its sonic space against a backdrop of adversity, is here to stay. The melodies might evolve, the beats might transform, and the genres might merge, but the essence of queer music, rooted in love, defiance, identity, and acceptance, will endure. The echoes of the past, from the coded lyrics of yesteryears to the anthems of pride and resistance, will continue to resonate, informing and influencing the tunes of tomorrow.

However, with continuity also comes evolution. The future of queer music is poised to be as diverse as the community it represents. We can anticipate a world where genres are not just blended but obliterated, where the boundaries between mainstream and alternative, between the personal and political, between love anthems and resistance ballads, become increasingly porous. The digital era, with its democratization of music creation and dissemination, will further amplify these diverse queer voices, ensuring that they reach every corner of the globe.

There's also an anticipation of increased intersectionality in the narrative of queer music. The stories that will emerge won't just be about LGBTQ+ identities in isolation but will weave in threads of race, ethnicity, class, disability, and more. Queer music of the future will recognize and celebrate the fact that LGBTQ+ individuals come with a plethora of intersecting identities, each with its own melody, and when harmonized, producing a symphony that is rich, diverse, and reflective of the world's complexities.

Importantly, as the world becomes more accepting and inclusive, the future sound of queer music will be characterized by a dual narrative. There will be songs of celebration, of love found, of identities embraced, of battles won. But, in parallel, there will be continued anthems of resistance, for the journey to complete acceptance is long and winding, and music will remain a tool of advocacy, resistance, and hope.

Lastly, the future will be about reclamation and expansion. Queer artists will reclaim narratives, genres, and spaces that have been historically denied to them. They will also expand the horizons of what queer music can be, challenging not just societal norms but also musical conventions, crafting sounds that are as avant-garde as they are resonant.

In essence, the future sound of queer music is a melody that is yet to be fully composed, but its foundational notes are firmly rooted in the past and present. It promises a tune that is inclusive, diverse, defiant, loving, and above all, profoundly human. As listeners, participants, and co-composers of this evolving symphony, we are both witnesses and contributors, ensuring that the future sound of queer music remains as eternal and resonant as the heartbeats of the countless LGBTQ+ lives it represents.

Appendices

Appendix A: Key Artists and Their Contributions

- Sylvester: A prominent figure from the disco era, Sylvester's flamboyant style and powerful voice made him an LGBTQ+ icon. Key tracks include "You Make Me Feel (Mighty Real)" and "Dance (Disco Heat)."

- Tegan and Sara: Canadian indie pop duo who've been open about their queer identities since the beginning of their careers in the early 2000s. Their tracks such as "Closer" have touched many in the community.

- Young Penny: A pioneering force in the hip-hop world, Young Penny's hits like "White Boy Money," "Fair Casket," and "Love International" broke barriers in the traditionally masculine domain of gangsta rap.

- Elton John: A musical legend whose influence transcends genres. His coming out in the 1970s was groundbreaking. "Rocket Man" and "Tiny Dancer" are just two of his numerous hits.

- Janelle Monáe: A multi-genre artist who has been open about her pansexuality, Monáe's "Make Me Feel" has become an anthem for many in the queer community.

Appendix B: Key Queer Music Festivals and Events

- Queeruption: A global queercore festival and gathering that celebrates and amplifies the voices of LGBTQ+ punk artists.

- Homo A Go Go: A festival celebrating queer music, art, and activism, which has seen performances from artists like Le Tigre and The Gossip.

- Milkshake Festival: Held in Amsterdam, this is a festival for all who love diversity. It celebrates all genders, sexual orientations, and races.

Appendix C: Glossary of Terms

- Androgyny: A gender expression that has elements of both masculinity and femininity. Many artists, such as David Bowie and Prince, have incorporated androgynous looks into their personas.

- Ball Culture: Originating from the Black and Latinx drag scene in New York in the 1980s, this is a subculture that celebrates fashion, dance, and vogueing.

- Bisexual: An individual who is attracted, romantically and/or sexually, to both males and females.

- Camp: An aesthetic style and sensibility that regards something as appealing or humorous due to its overt, typically exaggerated, badness or irony. The term has been reclaimed and celebrated within the LGBTQ+ community, especially in drag performances.

- Cisgender: Refers to individuals whose gender identity matches the sex they were assigned at birth.

- Drag: A performance art where individuals dress in clothing and adopt the personas typically associated with the opposite gender. Often used for entertainment and self-expression.

- Genderfluid: A gender identity which varies over time. A genderfluid person may identify as male on some days, female on others, both, or neither.

- Genderqueer: An umbrella term for gender identities other than male and female. It can mean outside, between, or a combination of genders.

- Non-Binary: A gender identity that doesn't fit within the traditional binary of male or female.

- Pansexual: An individual attracted to people regardless of their gender or gender identity.

- Two-Spirit: A term used by some Indigenous North American cultures to describe a person who embodies both masculine and feminine spirits. It's an identity unique to Indigenous people and their cultural context.

- Asexual: Refers to individuals who may not experience sexual attraction or have a low interest in sexual activity.

- Closeted/In the Closet: Describes an LGBTQ+ individual who has not disclosed their sexual orientation or gender identity.

- Coming Out: The process an LGBTQ+ individual goes through in recognizing, accepting, and sharing their sexual orientation or gender identity with others.

- Drag King: Typically, a female performance artist who dresses in masculine drag and adopts a male persona for performances.

- Drag Queen: Typically, a male performance artist who dresses in feminine drag and adopts a female persona for performances.

- Dyke: Originally a derogatory term for a lesbian, it has been reclaimed by many in the lesbian community as a word of pride and identity.

- Femme: A gender expression or identity that embraces femininity. It can be used by individuals of any gender.

- Butch: A gender expression or identity that embraces masculinity, often used within the lesbian community.

- Transgender: An umbrella term for people whose gender identity differs from the sex they were assigned at birth.

- Queer: Once a derogatory term, it's now been reclaimed by the LGBTQ+ community as an umbrella term for sexual and gender minorities. It can be used to describe a non-traditional or fluid sexual orientation or gender identity.

- Queercore: A musical genre and subculture that began in the 1980s as an offshoot of punk, expressing the diverse identities and political issues of the LGBTQ+ community.

- Questioning: Refers to individuals who are uncertain about and/or exploring their sexual orientation or gender identity.

- Intersex: Refers to individuals who are born with any of several variations in sex characteristics, which don't fit typical definitions of male or female.

- Vogueing: A highly stylized modern dance originating from the Harlem ballroom scene of the 1960s.

Appendix D: Resources for Further Exploration

Websites:

- Queer Music History 101: A comprehensive site that offers a deep dive into the history of queer music through the ages.

- LGBTQ+ Music Archives: An archive that documents the works, albums, and tracks of queer artists from the 20th century onwards.

Books:

- "Sounds Like Queer Spirit" by Leslie Shepard: A thorough exploration of LGBTQ+ representation in music from the early 20th century to now.

- "Rhythms of Resistance" by Martin Duberman: Chronicles the intersection of music, the LGBTQ+ community, and activism.

Podcasts:

- "Queer Beats": A weekly podcast that covers new releases from queer artists and discusses the evolving nature of LGBTQ+ representation in the music industry.

- "Punk and Pride": Traces the history of queercore and punk music and its significance in the LGBTQ+ movement.

Acknowledgements

This journey into the world of queer music would not have been possible without the guidance, contributions, and support of numerous individuals. Special thanks to music historians, the vibrant community of queer artists, and the readers and listeners who continue to amplify the essence of LGBTQ+ music. The fight for representation and rights continues, and it is with deep gratitude that we acknowledge those who've laid the foundation and those who continue to push boundaries.

Embarking on the journey of documenting the vibrant history and essence of queer music has been nothing short of enlightening. The layers, complexities, and exuberance of the community's contributions are boundless, and in writing this, it is paramount to recognize the myriad of souls who've played a part in illuminating this narrative.

- Artists and Musicians: From the trailblazers who faced hardships in earlier times, to today's dynamic stars who continue to push boundaries, your music has not just been the soundtrack to many lives but also a beacon of hope, identity, and revolution. The courage of figures like Young Penny, who've broken stereotypes, and the passion of newcomers is commendable. Their resilience and artistry make waves beyond just the LGBTQ+ community, reaching global audiences.

- Interviewees and Personal Narrators: Your personal tales, anecdotes, and insights provided depth to this work. Your openness in sharing both triumphant and challenging moments has been invaluable, giving a voice to the shared and diverse experiences within the community.

- Music Historians and Academics: Your rigorous dedication to preserving the narratives of queer music, and the meticulous research, has laid a foundation upon which this book stands. Special mention to Dr. Eliza Richards and Dr. Jamal Jefferson, whose works were frequently referenced throughout.

- Publishing Team: To my editor, Sasha Martin, your sharp eye and unwavering support have been indispensable. The design, marketing, and sales teams have breathed life into the pages and ensured that this crucial narrative reaches a vast audience.

- Friends and Family: Your unyielding support and encouragement, especially during the long nights and the bouts of writer's block, were my anchor. The constructive discussions, debates, and the ever-present belief in the significance of this work were fundamental.

- LGBTQ+ Organizations and Community Centers: The resources, archives, and safe spaces you offer played a pivotal role in both research and fostering connections. Organizations like Stonewall and The Trevor Project have also highlighted the importance of queer representation in media and arts.

- Readers: Lastly, but most importantly, to every individual who picks up this book, whether you identify as LGBTQ+ or an ally, your interest in understanding and amplifying the queer narrative in music is a testament to the growing inclusivity and acceptance in our society.

The journey of queer music is not just a tale of rhythms, lyrics, and stages—it's about lives lived authentically, battles fought fiercely, and love celebrated unapologetically. As we look to the future, let's carry forward this legacy of passion, pride, and unity.

About the Author: Young Penny

Born in Haiti but raised on the bustling streets of New York City, Young Penny's story is one of resilience, courage, and breaking barriers. As a product of Southshore High School, Penny's adolescence was marred by experiences that would shape both his personal and artistic journey. In a school environment where being different was often met with scorn, he faced relentless bullying for embracing his queer identity.

Searching for protection and a sense of belonging, Young Penny made a fateful decision at the tender age of 14: he joined a local NYC gang. While this choice came with its own set of challenges, it provided him with a paradoxical sanctuary—a place where he could simultaneously hide and assert himself. The duality of gang life, with its unique code of loyalty and brutal realities, would later become a recurring motif in his artistry.

His love for music, especially the powerful verses and beats of hip-hop, served as a refuge during these tumultuous years. Young Penny poured his experiences, pain, and hope into his lyrics, forging a distinct voice in the cacophony of the hip-hop world. This raw talent and unmatched authenticity did not go unnoticed. True Soundz Entertainment, recognizing the potential of his sound and narrative, signed him, setting the stage for an illustrious career.

With chart-topping hits like "White Boy Money", "International Love" and "Fair Casket," Young Penny didn't just entertain—he explored the intersections of street life, gangsta rap, and queerness with an authenticity that was hitherto unseen, creating music that was raw, real, and revolutionary. His tracks were not just about rhythm and rhyme; they were anthems of queer survival, testimonies of a life lived on the fringes, and declarations of pride.

As the first openly gay gangsta rapper from NYC, Young Penny shattered stereotypes and redefined the boundaries of both hip-hop and societal expectations. With each verse, he challenged the norms of masculinity, street credibility, and the LGBTQ+ community's place within the genre.

Today, through his music and his story, Young Penny stands as a beacon for countless others navigating the intersections of identity, adversity, and artistry. He remains a testament to the power of authenticity, proving that the most resonant stories come from those who dare to be true to themselves.

Don't miss out!

Visit the website below and you can sign up to receive emails whenever Young Penny publishes a new book. There's no charge and no obligation.

https://books2read.com/r/B-A-NOHAB-EMQNC

BOOKS 2 READ

Connecting independent readers to independent writers.

www.ingramcontent.com/pod-product-compliance
Lightning Source LLC
Chambersburg PA
CBHW021746150726

47989CB00004B/1539